A Practical Resource for Suppor Children's Right to Feel Safe

This programme of activities, created to be used alongside the storybook, *Something Has Happened*, has been designed to help children develop their own internal measure of safety, and teaches them how to ask for help if they feel unsafe.

The sessions and activities in this book directly correlate to episodes in the storybook *Something Has Happened*, covering the fundamental aspects of safeguarding as well as elements of the Protective Behaviours (PB) process. Taking adults and children through a wide range of discussion points and activities, all underpinned by clear guidance, it acts as a starting point to help children understand that being safe from harm is the most important right they have and that the trusted adults around them will always take action to believe and protect them.

Key features of this resource include:

- Session plans that directly link to events in the *Something Has Happened* storybook
- Clear, detailed and accessible activity plans that can be used with whole classes, small groups or with individual children
- Photocopiable activity sheets

With a concise and accessible introduction to the right to feel safe and Protective Behaviours, this is an invaluable resource for teachers, support staff and other professionals working with both primary and lower-secondary aged children.

Liz Bates is an independent education consultant. She supports both primary and secondary schools in all aspects of Emotional Health and Wellbeing, and Safeguarding, including whole school approaches, training staff and delivering talks to parents. Liz is a Protective Behaviours Trainer, a Wellbeing Award Advisor for Optimus and a regular contributor at national conferences.

A Practical Resource for Supporting Children's Right to Feel Safe

LIZ BATES
ILLUSTRATED BY NIGEL DODDS

Routledge
Taylor & Francis Group
LONDON AND NEW YORK

First published 2022
by Routledge
2 Park Square, Milton Park, Abingdon, Oxon OX14 4RN

and by Routledge
605 Third Avenue, New York, NY 10158

Routledge is an imprint of the Taylor & Francis Group, an informa business

British Library Cataloguing-in-Publication Data
A catalogue record for this book is available from the British Library

Library of Congress Cataloging-in-Publication Data
Names: Bates, Liz, author. | Dodds, Nigel (Archaeological illustrator) illustrator.
Title: A practical resource for supporting children's right to feel safe / Liz Bates ; Illustrated by Nigel Dodds.
Description: Abingdon, Oxon ; New York, NY : Routledge, 2022.
Identifiers: LCCN 2021020171 (print) | LCCN 2021020172 (ebook) | ISBN 9781032069159 (paperback) | ISBN 9781003204510 (ebook)
Subjects: LCSH: Security (Psychology) | Child abuse—Prevention. | Helping behavior.
Classification: LCC BF575.S35 B37 2022 (print) | LCC BF575.S35 (ebook) | DDC 155.9—dc23
LC record available at https://lccn.loc.gov/2021020171
LC ebook record available at https://lccn.loc.gov/2021020172

ISBN: 978-1-032-06915-9 (pbk)
ISBN: 978-1-003-20451-0 (ebk)

DOI: 10.4324/9781003204510

Typeset in Calibri
by codeMantra

Contents

Something Has Happened

Something Has Happened is a key resource for helping children to develop their own internal measure of safety rather than relying on external references. As adults we can be particularly good at telling children what is and is not safe – and rightly so. However equally, if not more important is children having the ability to understand and recognise for themselves safe and unsafe, and to know that if they feel unsafe, they need to seek help. Feeling safe and secure is central to children realising their potential and leading healthy and fulfilled lives, so giving them the opportunity to explore and understand the right to feel safe in its broadest sense is fundamental to their emotional health, resilience and wellbeing.

This book and resource is grounded in the fundamentals of Protective Behaviours and although a knowledge of Protective Behaviours is not necessary to make effective use of the resource, it will sit comfortably within any Protective Behaviours programme.

In the book we meet Joe. Something has happened to Joe – we never know what it is and that is important – it could be anything. This gives children the opportunity to talk about what might have happened. Children learn, with Joe, about how their bodies can tell them if they feel ok or not, what to do, who to tell, how to persist in order to get help and that we can break the rules in an emergency.

Recognising that feeling of 'unsafe' and being able to act on it is a lifelong skill that can be used from childhood and throughout adulthood.

We often don't even think about feeling safe – we take it for granted. It may not appear in our day to day language – if asked how we are feeling it is unlikely that we give the answer 'safe'. We only notice when there is an absence of feeling safe, when it is not there, when it has been replaced by a different feeling – feeling unsafe. We are also far more likely to call this something else too, rather than feeling unsafe. We may say anxious, scared, worried, threatened, unsure, nervous, isolated, different, picked on…

The storybook and related activities explore how Joe knows that something is wrong – here we unpick what safe and unsafe mean, how they feel and how important it is if we feel unsafe to talk to a trusted person. Understanding how safe feels will help children to choose a trusted person because it will be someone they feel safe with. The safety continuum introduces children to what exists between safe and unsafe such as 'fun to feel scared' and 'risking on purpose'. The book then goes on to ask who might be on Joe's network of

DOI: 10.4324/9781003204510-1

trusted adults – who they might be, why he might choose them, how he can approach and tell them, and what might happen afterwards. The book also looks at breaking the rules – in an emergency, interrupting adults, persisting until someone listens and even lying can be lifesaving. This resource can be used with all children, regardless of what it is that causes them to feel unsafe; including those children who may not need the skills now but might do in the future.

Safeguarding

Disclosure is the process by which a child will let someone know that abuse is taking place. Sometimes this is direct, sometimes this is indirect.

Direct disclosure is when a child makes a specific statement about something that has happened or is happening to them.

Indirect disclosure is more ambiguous and less specific, but it is something that a child may do or say which indicates or implies that something is wrong.

As this book is designed to help children to tell a trusted adult, possibly about significant harm, it cannot be overstated how important your Safeguarding procedures are and how critical it is that you know and follow them.

When receiving a disclosure of potentially significant harm you should:

- **Listen**
- **Be neutral – not shocked**
- **Believe the child**
- **Stay calm**
- **Reassure the child that they have done the right thing**
- **Don't make any promises – to make it better, to make it go away, and most importantly, to keep it secret**
- **You may ask open questions – but only to establish your level of concern. You are not investigating and should not ask closed / leading questions**
- **Explain what will happen next – which is**
  - **You will inform the Designated Safeguarding Lead (DSL)**
- **Make a record at the earliest opportunity – these may be handwritten notes of what the child said, or your setting may use MyConcern or CPOMS or similar**
- **Know your limit – you are establishing a concern, not investigating**

It is important to say here that for most children disclosure of significant harm is not something they will ever need to do. However, for those children who need to and who do, our correct response is crucial.

Consequently, although this resource may help a child to disclose significant harm, it is of benefit to all children by emphasising their right to feel safe.

When we look at what is known about abuse of children when it is happening and compare that to adults disclosing abuse done to them as children, it becomes clear that disclosing abuse as a child when it is happening, is an extraordinarily difficult step to take.

Protecting children from harm (**Children's Commissioner Nov 2015**) suggests that approximately 1 in 8 victims of Child Sexual Abuse come to the attention of statutory agencies. So for every child who discloses there are 7 children not saying anything.

It is not difficult to imagine why this is the case. But I believe it comes down to 5 key elements:

Who to tell – is there an adult that I really trust, that I feel really safe with?

When to tell – will this adult listen to me or are they too busy?

How to tell – what are the words I need to say this?

Is it safe to tell – what will happen if I tell? Will I get in trouble? Will someone else get in trouble?

Is it worth telling – will this hurting stop if I tell? Will I be believed?

If you are an adult working with children, you will know that you have a responsibility for Safeguarding. A child may choose you as the person they feel safest with and so make a disclosure to you. Knowing, understanding and acting on your organisation's Safeguarding procedures is the most important role you have.

However, no child will disclose unless they feel safe enough to do so and as many as possible of those 5 key elements are in place. This resource is designed to meet the needs of each of these elements.

We know from historical cases dependent on disclosure that 'telling' as a child does not happen easily, automatically or obviously. And although as adults we are so much better at listening and believing, there could still be as many as 7 out of 8 children who are not 'telling'.

Disclosure of abuse is the most extreme end of a continuum whereby a child may need to tell a trusted adult about something which is upsetting, frightening or disrupting their life in some way. This could be at home, at school, in the virtual world or in the real world and along that continuum, to name but a few, are: being bullied, threatened, groomed, coerced, teased, picked on, left out, isolated.

Feeling safe enough to tell someone is necessary in all these instances.

Moving both children and parents on from 'stranger danger' is critical. When working with parents I still find this often tops the list when they are asked what they do to keep their child safe, and yet we know that children are at far greater risk of harm from people they know than from strangers. And there is a real dichotomy around the meaning of 'friend' and 'knowing' someone on the internet. A parent may feel their child needs protecting from 'strangers' on the internet, whilst the child believes they are interacting with 'friends', albeit friends they have never met in the real world.

There is also much to be done regarding keeping secrets and discussing with children the dangers of complying with someone who tells them, "never tell anyone about this", whether it is by a person they know well or not. Having choice and control is covered in depth later in this resource, relating it to coercion and persuasion.

Protective Behaviours

Based on Protective Behaviours and underpinned by **the right to feel safe,** this resource is relevant to all areas of Safeguarding and can be used with a whole class, a group or as a one-to-one intervention. What a child learns from this resource may not be needed by them today, but they can draw from it for the rest of their lives.

Protective Behaviours is an internationally recognised process and a practical approach to personal safety that teaches understanding and strategies to recognise and act on unsafe feelings and experiences. This approach is 'profound in its simplicity' and can be **'taught to anyone irrespective of age, ability, gender, race'** ('The Protective Behaviours Process: Principles and Strategies' Maria Huffer, Managing Director Protective Behaviours Consortium CIC (PBC)). This resource is influenced by the Protective Behaviours approach and draws on elements of its teaching to create an accessible and valuable addition to Safeguarding for all children and young people.

The sessions in this resource reflect the following areas of Protective Behaviours:

We all have the right to feel safe all the time – Theme 1

Early Warning Signs

The Safety Continuum

We can talk with someone about anything even if it's awful or small – Theme 2

Networks

Persistence

Risking on Purpose

One Step Removed

Please note this resource is not a complete programme of Protective Behaviours.

Preparation

Before using this resource, I would like to invite you, the adult, to reflect on the position taken by you and by your setting on being and feeling safe. I have worked with many hundreds of schools and other settings and most of them will at some point ask their children if they feel safe. What few of them do is ensure that the children understand what feeling safe means, what it feels like and the fact that **feeling** safe can be quite different to **being** safe. It is very possible to **be** safe but not **feel** safe (we will look at this later in the resource). We cannot expect children to tell us if they feel safe if they do not know what safe feels like.

Reflection

If at all possible, share these reflection activities with your colleagues.

What do you do in your organisation/setting to help children to be safe?

You will probably think about: child protection and safeguarding procedures, health and safety, security locks, IDs, upkeep of equipment, risk assessments, following up absences, emergency contacts, numerous policies, epi-pen training … the list goes on.

Now consider a slightly different question.

What do you do in your organisation/setting to help children to **feel** safe?

This requires another way of thinking – this is to do with relationships, language, actions, facial expressions, time, patience, understanding, knowledge, empathy, mentalising...

Smiling at a child and asking how they are is the starting point.

But whatever your list, I would add to it - helping a child to understand what feeling safe means.

They cannot tell us if they feel safe or unsafe if they do not know what safe and unsafe *feel* like, and it is not the same for each of them, or indeed for us.

Emotional safety is not necessarily a direct outcome of physical safety, although of course important. Understanding the emotional barriers to disclosure - shame, fear of getting into trouble, speaking badly of parents/wanting to protect family members/friends etc, will enable an exploration of what may support a child's disclosure.

The first part of the book and resource interrogates what is actually meant by the word safe, feeling safe and unsafe, and establishing the difference between unsafe and its 'cousins' fun to feel scared and risking on purpose.

The Protective Behaviours' language of safe and unsafe is used throughout this book and resource but it is likely that children will use other words to describe these feelings: (see the first activity in Session 1)

Safe – happy, relaxed, smiley, I belong, warm, having friends...

Unsafe – alone, hurt, bullied, hungry, frightened...

How many words can you and your colleagues come up with?

It is also useful to discuss with colleagues all the reasons why a child might feel unsafe. Doing this as an activity brings the realisation of just how many and varied the reasons are.

They may be reasons from home – insecure attachment, domestic abuse, neglect, mental health issues, bereavement, other trauma or Adverse Childhood Experiences (ACE).

They may be reasons from school – additional educational needs, peer abuse / bullying, friendship issues, a newly arrived child.

And when are the times when these feelings arise? – arriving, going home, talking to an adult, breaktime, lunchtime, maths, PE, sitting next to…., sitting on my own, asking to go to the toilet, making friends, reading aloud, answering a question, being alone, being in a group…

(None of the above are definitive lists.)

The Children You Work With

If you have responsibility for, or work with, looked-after children it is possible that their experience of safe and unsafe may be heightened and very specific. Many of these children will have experienced fear, harm and disruption and may never have felt safe enough to talk about those experiences. In schools the designated teacher for looked-after and previously looked-after children has a crucial role in developing support for and understanding of these children, part of which must be creating safe and secure places and relationships within a school setting.

These children are at one end of a continuum of need and at the other are children who may experience life events that are less traumatic but nonetheless will encounter fears, worries and incidents which will impact on their sense of safety, be it falling out with friends, the death of a pet, bullying, isolation. *Something Has Happened*, the storybook and resource, can provide a structure to recognise need and access support which is of value to all.

The function of any adult in a position of trust is to listen to, believe and support children.

"Safeguarding is everyone's responsibility …

… Anyone working with children should see and speak to the child; listen to what they say; take their views seriously…": *Working Together to Safeguard Children* (HM Government).

The voice of the child has to be at the centre of any actions taken by the adults around them, but all of this is entirely dependent on a child

- knowing that what is happening to them is not ok
- knowing that they do not feel safe – when that is happening, with that person…
- knowing they can do something about it and knowing what that is

- feeling safe enough to tell someone
- knowing who to tell, how to tell, when to tell, that it is safe to tell, that it is worth telling, and then telling.

This resource pack is written in an order that provides a consecutive process although some of the activities can be used as discrete sessions. You will know the children best and can use the materials in a way that is most suitable – extending or shortening sessions where necessary. You may choose to ignore the 'Sessions' format and just work through at your own pace.

Some activities will take longer than others, so be as flexible as you are able.

This resource can both support your (the adult) understanding of Safeguarding, and how to work collaboratively with children in identifying when they may not feel safe and supporting disclosure, and what safeguarding may look like 'on the ground'. That collaborative nature enables a shared language to develop between children and adults, further supporting the opportunity for pupils to build positive relationships with staff/adults which will promote effective safeguarding. The *process* of using this resource will in turn encourage more valuable safeguarding. This resource can be picked up by any staff member within a setting, such as a school, and promotes learning both for adults and children.

Format

Throughout the resource the following are used:

Plain text – indicates information and descriptions of the process for you, the adult.

Italic text – verbatim instructions, questions, guidance and explanations which you can read / speak directly to the children if you wish.

Finally

There is nothing in this resource that applies to children only. Everything that is covered is just as relevant to an adult who feels unsafe as it is to a child. Please remember you too have **the right to feel safe**.

Liz Bates

lizslamer@gmail.com
Something Has Happened

Session 1
Feeling Safe

This session introduces an understanding of what feeling safe actually feels like.

As with every session concerned with how we feel or what we think about things, it is really important to reinforce that we can and do all feel differently about things. Later sessions will explore this in more detail.

Discussion Activity

What do we mean by the word safe?

It is likely that children will talk about being safe initially.

Possible answers – not in danger, looked after, okay, not going to get hurt, with people I like, with my friends, with my family, happy, loved, not talking to strangers, or perhaps a box that we lock money in...

How does safe feel?

A trickier question but try to steer the children towards some physical feelings – warm, snuggly, liked, smiley, relaxed, belonging – they may also repeat some of the previous answers.

Read page 1 of the *Something Has Happened* storybook.

DOI: 10.4324/9781003204510-2

Discussion Activity

What might have happened to Joe?

In pairs or small groups children discuss together and then feed back their suggestions.

Children to share their suggestions. If there are disagreements, remind them that we can all feel differently about things and you will come back to this later.

Possible answers – he's being bullied, he's broken friends, he's lost something, he got into trouble, been hit, mum and dad are arguing, forgot his homework...

All suggestions are valid.

Read pages 2 and 3 of the *Something Has Happened* storybook.

Joe has got some feelings in his body. These feelings happen when we feel unsafe.

Activity – Joe's Feelings

Each child to have a body outline (**Appendix 1**) and draw on pictures of Joe's feelings of butterflies in his tummy and his heart beating fast.

Can they think of other feelings Joe might be having in his body?

Draw on pictures of those feelings.

These could be:

> Jelly legs, feeling sick, wanting to go to the toilet, feeling very hot or cold, shaking all over...

Activity – How are you feeling?

To create some physiological responses in a safe environment.

In the following activities the idea is not to win or guess correctly but to recognise and record the feelings of anticipation, excitement, nervousness which will naturally start to happen. Please avoid saying 'how does this make you feel?'; rather, say 'how are you feeling?'.

A giant Jenga game – if you are able to set this up. As each child approaches to remove a block ask them to say aloud what they are feeling, what is happening to their body.

A feely box – as each child approaches the box and puts their hands in ask them to say aloud what they are feeling, what is happening to their body.

Blow up a balloon – ask the children what they are feeling.

(There are other simple activities – a jack-in-the-box, reading 'Going on a Bear Hunt', playing hide and seek, anything that creates feelings of anticipation of a surprise or the unknown.)

Draw together any other feelings that were experienced. These can then be drawn on the figure outline.

*We call these feelings our **Early Warning Signs (EWS)**. They are signs and signals that our bodies produce automatically. They are a natural response when we feel uncertain or nervous or anxious, threatened, or frightened. It is the body's way of telling us to be careful, to be aware of danger, that everything might not be okay, that we might not be safe, and they are very important.*

(There is much more on this in the storybook *Myg and Me* and resource *My Brilliant Brain*.)

So now we know that Joe's body is sending him Early Warning Signs telling him that everything is not okay and he might not be safe.

We are going to think about ways to help Joe. (If you have any good ideas bring them along to the next session / lesson / meeting.)

We have been describing Joe's physical feelings. There are other sorts of feelings too.

Emotional feelings like happiness or anger.

Activity – Feelings Alphabet

Create an alphabet of feelings words to display in the class.

Children can work in pairs or small groups to do their own first of all and then share to make one for the class / group.

See **Appendix 2** for some suggestions.

Some letters are really tricky so allow lots of latitude and creativity. This alphabet can then be a great reminder / reinforcement of feelings language, introducing a wider emotional vocabulary.

At the end of this session give the children the opportunity to relax and be calm, to move on from thinking about Joe and his EWS. You could do a relaxation exercise or play some calming music. This is a great way to end *every* session. For some ideas see *Appendix 16*.

(For much more on anxiety, calming and self-regulation see the *My Brilliant Brain* resource and *Myg and Me* storybook.)

Session 2
My Safety Scale

This session introduces the idea of safety along a continuum – in Protective Behaviours called The Safety Continuum. We can often **feel** unsafe even when we **are** safe and sometimes we enjoy those feelings.

We can all feel differently about the same thing; we can feel differently at different times; we can feel differently to someone else. (There is lots more on this in the storybook and resource *Feel, Think and Do with Ruby, Rafa and Riz*.) Our Early Warning Signs can show up at any time along the continuum.

> **Read pages 4 and 5 of the *Something Has Happened* storybook.**

Discuss what happened and Joe's feelings.

Just like playing Jenga or using the feely box, Joe does some things for fun and he gets the same feelings. So that seems a bit confusing. How come we get the same feelings when we are doing something for fun and when we are unsafe?

When Joe is riding his bike downhill he can say 'this is fun to feel scared'. He gets some of those EWS, those feelings in his tummy or his heart beating fast, but it feels like fun.

When Joe is reading in assembly, it's not fun, he is nervous, but it is exciting and a bit risky because he could make a mistake. He can say 'I'm risking on purpose' because he wants to do it. He gets some of those EWS, those feelings of being a bit shaky or his legs feeling like jelly and it is OK because he knows it will stop.

So Joe knows he is still safe when he does those things.

When Joe starts his new school do you think he is feeling safe, fun to feel scared, risking on purpose or unsafe?

Expect different answers – that shows how we can feel differently about the same thing.

DOI: 10.4324/9781003204510-3

When Joe is gaming with his friends do you think he is feeling safe, fun to feel scared, risking on purpose or unsafe?

Ask the children to explain their answers.

Activity – My Safety Scale

This activity puts the safety scale into practice.

You will need a large enough space for children to move around and stand near their chosen card.

If you prefer or do not have access to space or you are working with an individual child, you can do this activity on paper using **Appendix 3**. The child can mark their position on the scale after each situation. They could use a coloured dot or a word or tiny picture to indicate each situation.

This activity includes 'Risking on Purpose' so it is important to discuss what the children understand by taking a risk.

Answers to look for – doing something that might be scary, doing something that might not turn out well, something that they have never done before, a brave thing, something they need to pluck up courage to do, afterwards they are glad they did it.

It is also important to emphasise the difference between taking a risk that can be exciting, life changing or life-saving and harmful risk taking that can be dangerous.

This continuum / scale uses 'Risking on Purpose' as a decision that is made to do something which we may not enjoy or are scared by, but we want to do it and we have choice and control over it (see below).

Use **Appendix 4** cards Feeling Safe, Fun to Feel Scared, Risking on Purpose, Feeling Unsafe and **Appendix 5** Safety Scale Situations.

Lay out the 4 cards in a line with enough space to allow children to move around and in between the cards.

Read aloud the first situation and ask the children to stand by the card that represents how they think they would feel doing that. It doesn't matter if they have actually done it or not. Initially you may find that children will stand by their friend, but as you go through more situations, they will often choose to show that they feel differently. It helps if you join in and show that it is okay to feel differently.

After the third situation begin to ask them to say why they are standing in a particular place and reinforce how differently people feel about the same thing. Repeat this for subsequent situations. These are all opportunities for them to talk about and share their feelings and to consider that what is fun for them might not be fun for someone else.

*Most of the time when we get these feelings, our Early Warning Signs or 'uh oh' feelings, we are having scary fun or taking a safe risk and that is fine **AS LONG AS***

- ***I have chosen what I am doing** – I want to and have chosen to go on a roller coaster*
- ***I can control or stop what I am doing** – I can switch off a scary film if I am not enjoying it*
- ***I know it is going to stop** – when I read in assembly I know it will only be for a few minutes*

It is these 3 things – Choice, Control and Time Limit – that tell us that we are still safe even if our bodies think otherwise!

It is important to note here that a child using the internet unsafely, for example being coerced into a dangerous behaviour such as taking and sharing inappropriate selfies or talking intimately with someone they haven't met, may feel like 'Fun to Feel Scared' or 'Risking on Purpose'. However, the child is not in control if they are being persuaded or pushed or threatened by another person to do things they wouldn't otherwise do.

Activity – I Feel Safe When...

Each child to have a copy of **Appendix 6** I Feel Safe When... . Read through the wording together to reinforce the information and then they can draw a picture to represent an action or situation for themselves. Or they can make their own, copy into a workbook – whatever works best, but ensure they copy the wording and talk it through.

Calm Time. Relaxation or calm music.

Session 3
Let's Help Joe

Read page 6 of the *Something Has Happened* storybook.

So now we can see that Joe doesn't feel safe because he isn't having fun, he hasn't chosen it, he doesn't want to feel like this and he doesn't know if it will stop.

This is how Joe knows he doesn't feel safe.

Read page 7 of the *Something Has Happened* storybook.

Discussion Activity

What things do we do to help us feel better if we are sad, or scared? What do we do to take our minds off things?

Children can discuss in small groups to begin with and then open it out.

You might get these answers – forget about it, pretend it doesn't matter. If so, it will be valuable to talk about why that might not work, and this is covered below.

If anyone suggests talking to a friend or an adult – say *'Brilliant suggestion, I think that will be a big help to Joe. Let's see what happens.'*

Activity

Draw up a Top 5 or Top 10 activities or things Joe could try. **Appendix 7** has some suggestions.

Do they always work? Can anyone give an example of doing an activity to take their mind off something else and, like Joe, it not working?

DOI: 10.4324/9781003204510-4

Read pages 8 and 9 of the *Something Has Happened* storybook.

Discussion Activity

What does it mean if Joe's feelings don't go away? If he can't forget about what has happened?

You are looking for – it's important, it's a big thing, he's really upset / hurt / frightened / in trouble, he can't sort it out by himself, he needs help.

Even if Joe pretends it doesn't matter, deep inside it still matters because his feelings aren't going away.

So what else can we suggest?

If earlier discussion produced suggestions of asking an adult or a friend remind them of that. If not, ask for more suggestions of what Joe could do.

What might happen if Joe doesn't tell someone or ask for help?

The problem might get worse. Joe might feel worse.

Joe needs to do something.

Read pages 10 and 11 of the *Something Has Happened* storybook.

So when Joe has these EWS that don't go away this tells him something is wrong. He can:

Stop – *interrupt what he is doing.*

Feel – *listen to what his body is telling him. Feelings are like a language without words.*

Think – *what can he do?*

Act – *speak to someone he trusts.*

Write this up on the IWB or flipchart. If the children are keeping a workbook they can write this there.

Read page 12 of the *Something Has Happened* storybook.

Discussion Activity

Why do you think Joe has chosen these people?

Encourage the children to move beyond 'he trusts them'.

What does it mean to trust someone?

How do you know you trust someone?

How do you feel when you are with someone you trust?

The fundamental response to this final question must be "when I am with this person I feel comfortable, happy, relaxed, … safe".

Who else could someone put on their network?

Allow children to name as many people / roles as possible. Remind them that a suggestion may be right for one person but not necessarily for everyone. (Please remember that for some children Mum or Dad may not be who they want on their network.) Whilst we would encourage children to have adults on a network, it is important that they can include a friend too if they choose. Friends have an important role to play – their help can be: going with the child to tell an adult; speaking to an adult on the child's behalf; being there to listen; helping to suggest a trusted adult from their own network (borrowing someone's network can be extremely valuable if a child is struggling to make their own).

Possible suggestions:

Family member, foster mum, friend, carer, social worker, teacher, learning mentor, counsellor, lunch-time supervisor, therapist, neighbour, friend's mum….

Activity – Our Network Tree

Using the Leaf Template (**Appendix 8**) pupils write suggestions of who someone might have on their network:

mum, dad, nanna, uncle (other family members), police officer, lollipop lady, brownie pack leader (other club staff), child minder, religious leader… (and the list mentioned above).

The 'leaves' can then be displayed as a network tree. This can help to give children suggestions of people they may not have thought of.

Read pages 13–16 of the *Something Has Happened* storybook.

Discuss Joe's reasons for choosing the people on his network.

Recap on discussion of what it means to trust someone.

If we trust someone, we feel safe with them. They will not hurt us. They will not let us down.

Like Joe when we choose our network, we can pick someone who is:

A good listener, a problem solver.

Reliable, knowledgeable.

Helpful, knows other people who are helpful.

Sympathetic.

Someone I can contact easily.

Will believe me. Will take action for me and with me. Will not let me down.

Someone I feel safe with.

But how do we know?

There are lots of ways we can know if someone has those qualities.

- *I have a close relationship with them so I know them really well, like Joe did with Dad*
- *I have seen them helping others, like Joe did with Aneeta*
- *I know it is their job, like a social worker*
- *Someone else has told me how helpful they are, like Joe did with Ms Lopez*
- *They have helped me before, like Joe did with Mr Cooper*
- *I feel safe with them – I have no Early Warning Signs when I am with them.*

Important

You may get EWS if you are about to talk with a trusted person. These EWS are not about the person you are with – you have already chosen them because you feel safe with them – the EWS are because you are about to take a safe risk, risking on purpose – the risk of telling. It is a risk because there is something that worries you, scares you, or upsets you and it seems very scary to talk about it. But remember the person you are telling is someone who will not hurt you – that is why you chose them.

Calm Time. Relaxation or calm music.

Session 4
My Network

If this session does not follow straight on from Session 3, please spend some time re-capping networks. Look at the network tree again; remind the children what 'trusted adult' means; what it means to trust someone; what they want from a 'trusted adult' and how they might know someone has those qualities.

Activity – My Network

Children create their own network. They could have two networks – one of trusted adults and one of friends, or a combined network. **Appendix 9** has a model template showing you what to include and a blank template that can be copied, or children can draw around their own hand. They can then write the names of the people they have chosen.

There may be children who will struggle to think of anyone. It is important that you become that trusted adult for them. This will not happen immediately – the child may need evidence of your trustworthiness. If they are still reluctant to use you, suggest that you go on as their emergency network. Just in case.

Also ensure that they all have emergency contact numbers such as

Emergency services 999
Childline 0800 1111
Social worker (if appropriate)

Each child can then make the network bookmark using **Appendix 10**.

Activity – Network Invitation

A child will need to tell their chosen trusted adults that they have been chosen to be on the child's network. This may be difficult for the child to explain so having a Network Invitation enables the information to be

---

DOI: 10.4324/9781003204510-5

passed on in a concise and easily understood way. Sharing and explaining networks will take away some of the anxiety and EWS attached to disclosing or simply sharing a worry. Having their feelings and concerns dismissed, trivialised or invalidated is a sure way to stop a child, indeed anyone, from seeking help in the future so having the invitation to help to explain how important this is can be extremely valuable.

To help them explain what being on their network means, they can use **Appendix 11**, design their own Network Invitation, or you could have a competition and choose one to copy for the whole class.

Calm Time. Relaxation or calm music.

Session 5
Don't Give Up

Read pages 17–19 of the *Something Has Happened* storybook.

Discuss what has happened.

Joe has shown persistence by asking more than one person.
Persistence means to try and try and try again and it can be very important.
There are times when persistence is important such as in an emergency, like Joe.
There are times when it is not so important!

Activity – Persistence Cards

Using **Appendix 12** - Persistence Cards, this activity can be done as a whole class or group, in small groups, pairs or individually.

Display cards one by one or give small groups a set to work through.

Look at each card and decide if this is an emergency where Joe might need to persist, or a time when perhaps Joe should stop asking. The children should also think about 'why'?

After going through the cards, open up the discussion for children to share their decisions, their reasons why and give their own examples of when to persist and when not to.

Discussion Activity

Joe has persisted but all the people on his network are busy and Joe feels like giving up.

Should he give up?

Why?

Explore any answers that suggest Joe should just forget about it and go away because he has tried everyone.

He can try another day.

Is that a safe thing for Joe to do?

Why not?

Look for answers that identify that Joe needs help.

We have seen that Joe's feelings aren't going away, we know that he does not feel safe. This tells us that Joe cannot manage this on his own.

Read pages 20–22 of the *Something Has Happened* storybook.

Discuss what has happened.

What do Josh and Sophie suggest to Joe?

Breaking the rules by interrupting Ms Lopez.

'Children shouldn't interrupt adults if they are busy or talking'. This is an unwritten rule that we often give to children but one that can be challenged.

In an emergency interrupting someone, anyone, can be lifesaving.

A flashing blue light and a siren on an ambulance is a way of interrupting.

A fire alarm is an interruption.

They are there to make people notice and know that there is an emergency.

Joe interrupting Ms Lopez might be breaking an unwritten rule but it tells Ms Lopez that this is important, an emergency for Joe.

It is ok to break the rules in an emergency.

Other rules we can break in an emergency:

Telling lies – if Joe was being bullied and teased and dared to go into a shop to steal something he could lie and say he had a dentist appointment so had to get home really quickly.

(Please note here that there is an opportunity for covering saying no to an adult or older child. Adult survivors of childhood abuse have reported saying they wished they could have said 'no' to the abuser and walked away. However, this will need specific circumstances and to fit within your Safeguarding arrangements so it is not part of this session.)

Remember the Safety Scale?
Remember Risking on Purpose?
Joe is risking on purpose by breaking an unwritten rule. He is nervous and anxious but he really wants to do it.

Joe is risking on purpose by interrupting Ms Lopez.

Activity – Being a Helpful Friend

Using **Appendix 13** – Being a Helpful Friend

Do you remember when we did our networks, we talked about why we might have a friend on our network?

What can a helpful friend do?

Go with you to tell an adult.

Speak to an adult for you.

Listen to you.

Suggest a trusted adult to share from their network.

Remind you it's ok to break the rules in an emergency.

Josh and Sophie are helpful friends.

Children to work in pairs or small groups initially working through the situations in **Appendix 13**. Imagine each situation was happening to a friend – agree on an action, a deed or what they could say that would make them a helpful friend. The situations require a range of responses, including helping a friend who has chosen an unwise or unsafe action or behaviour.

Open out the discussion to share the responses.

(There is much more on kindness in the *Cool to be Kind* storybook and resource pack.)

Calm Time. Relaxation or calm music.

Session 6
Feeling Safer

Read pages 23–27 of the *Something Has Happened* storybook.

Discuss what happens.

Joe is listened to by Ms Lopez. His feelings are accepted. His worries are believed.

Ms Lopez will try and help. This does not mean that Ms Lopez will be able to fix everything or make everything better or make all Joe's worries go away, but she will do what she can. She may have to speak to another trusted adult. And talking to her means that Joe is not on his own anymore. He has a trusted adult on his side.

Knowing this can help Joe to feel calmer and happier and safer.

Trusted adults will always do everything they can to help. If they don't or can't then choose another trusted adult from your network. Or borrow from your friend's network. Or use your emergency numbers.

Key learning

Go through each of these steps to ensure that children understand each point.

Did Joe know who to tell?
Yes, he knew to tell someone on his network.

Did Joe know how to tell?
Yes, Joe knew that it was ok to talk about his feelings (see also 'Other Ways to Tell' activity below).

Did Joe know when to tell?
Yes, Joe knew it was important to tell someone as soon as possible even if he had to interrupt.

DOI: 10.4324/9781003204510-7

Did Joe know that it was safe to tell?
Yes, because Joe was telling a trusted adult with whom he felt safe.

Did Joe know that it was worth telling?
Yes, because he knew Ms Lopez had helped other children in his class.

Did Joe keep trying?
Yes, Joe persisted until he started to feel safe again.

Activity – Other Ways To Tell

Having adults who notice is a key feature of Safeguarding. It is often much easier for a child to respond to an adult who has noticed something is wrong and gently asks them how they are feeling or if they can help, rather than have to begin a disclosure themselves. (There is more on this in *Feel Think and Do with Ruby, Rafa and Riz.*) Having a way to indicate that they are not feeling ok instead of having to say it out loud can be of help for some children.

It might be that a child needs a non-verbal way of indicating that they feel unsafe / worried / scared / alone…

Remember it is important to be able to contact the people on your network. Sometimes it can be hard to start a conversation with an adult, even a trusted adult, and that is ok, a trusted adult will understand this. It can help to have another way of indicating how you are feeling, or that you want to talk to a trusted adult.

Each child can create a set of Feeling Faces.

3 pieces of card with a different face on each.

A smiley (feeling safe) face

 or  or  or or something similar

An 'ok' face

 or

A worried or sad (feeling unsafe) face

 or or or

The child can then display the appropriate card indicating how they are feeling:

At the start of the day

At the start of a session

At the start of a meeting

At home

They can:

Put the card on the classroom display / feelings wall next to their name with everyone else

Put the card on their table for you to see

Hand the card to you

Or you may think of other ways that may work better for your setting.

This means that at the start of each day you can see how the children are feeling and use it as an opportunity to ask how they are feeling and if they would like to talk with you.

Or each child could have a set of 'traffic lights' cards.

Green – safe

Amber – OK at the moment

Red – unsafe

And put these on the desk or table, or hand to you during the course of the day.

You may use a worry box which can be a valuable strategy. However, it is important to note that a worry box must be opened every day. A child may put a worry in the box which indicates they are at risk of significant harm and believe their worry will be seen on the same day. This can be potentially harmful if the worry is not acknowledged and possibly not acted on.

Activity – My Feeling Safe Safe

Appendix 14 – My Safe Safe

Each child to have a copy of the safe on *Appendix 14* and draw or write in words, objects, names … anything that helps them to feel safe.

A piece of music
A cuddly toy
A stress ball
A cup of hot chocolate
A favourite book
A family member's name or picture
Their pet's name or picture
Their friends' names or pictures
Anything else?

We all have the right to feel safe all the time – Protective Behaviours Theme 1.

As adults working with children, we have a responsibility to those children, to uphold their right to feel safe and support them in achieving that.

We can talk with someone about anything even if it is awful or small – Protective Behaviours Theme 2.

Are you that someone for the children you work with? Why and how have they chosen you? And how do you know they have chosen you?

I hope that by working through this resource you feel able to support the children you come into contact with to know what to do if they feel unsafe.

And to display in your classroom or workroom, clubhouse or office:

"We all have the right to feel safe and the responsibility to uphold the rights of others to feel safe."

Liz Bates
lizslamer@gmail.com

Appendix 1: Body Outline

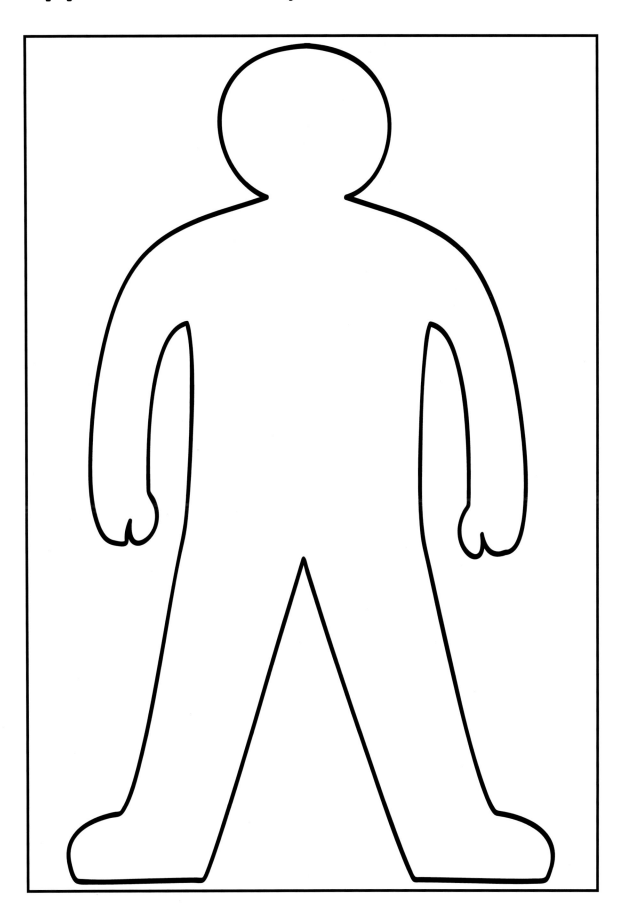

Appendix 2: Feelings Alphabet

These can be emotional or physical feelings:

A – AMUSED / ANGRY
B – BRAVE / BORED / BUTTERFLIES
C – CALM / CONFUSED
D – DELIGHTED / DISAPPOINTED
E – EAGER / EMBARRASSED
F – FRIENDLY / FURIOUS / FIDGETY
G – GRATEFUL / GUILTY
H – HOPEFUL / HOPELESS
I – IMPORTANT / ISOLATED
J – JOYFUL / JEALOUS / JELLY LEGS
K – KIND / 'KRANKY'
L – LOVING / LONELY
M – MOTIVATED / MUDDLED
N – NICE / NIGGLY
O – OK / OVERWHELMED
P – PLEASED / PANTS
Q – QUIET / QUESTIONING / QUICK BREATHING
R – RELAXED / RESENTFUL
S – STRONG / SAD / SWEATY
T – THRILLED / TERRIFIED
U – UNIQUE / UNCOMFORTABLE
V – VALUED / VILE
W – WONDERFUL / WORRIED
X – EXCITED / EXHAUSTED
Y – YAAAYYY / YAWNY
Z – ZANY / ZONKED

Appendix 3: My Safety Scale

Put a picture in each box to show each step on **your** Safety Scale. For example, you could put playing with friends in the Feeling Safe box; reading a scary story in Fun to Feel Scared box; jumping off the high board in Risking on Purpose; being alone in the dark in Feeling Unsafe. Remember it is up to you and can be different from everyone else.

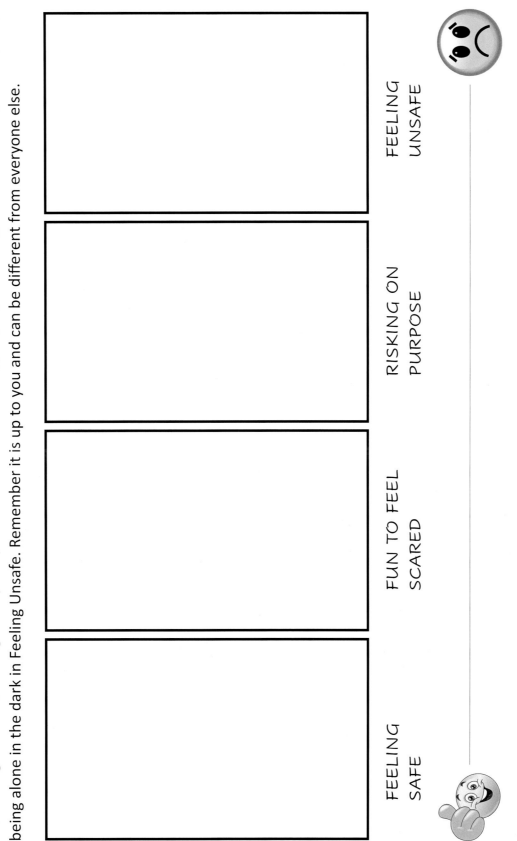

FEELING
SAFE

FUN TO FEEL
SCARED

RISKING ON
PURPOSE

FEELING
UNSAFE

Mark on the Safety Scale how you think you might feel. You can use a different picture, colour, symbol or word each time.

Appendix 4: Safety Scale Cards

> # Feeling Safe

> # Fun to Feel Scared

Risking on Purpose

Feeling Unsafe

Appendix 5: Safety Scale Situations

Please adjust and add to suit the children you are working with.

Putting your hands in a feely box

Falling out with a friend

Riding a roller coaster

Speaking in assembly

Singing a solo

Watching a scary film

Opening a birthday present

Keeping a secret

Walking on a tightrope

Riding a bike really fast

Jumping off the high board at the pool

Answering a question in class

Being in the dark

Reading messages on my phone

Holding a snake

Appendix 6: I Feel Safe When...

I have chosen what I
am doing even if it is
fun to feel scared

I can control or stop
what I am doing if I
feel unsafe

I know it is going
to stop even if I am
risking on purpose

Appendix 7: Top 10 Activities

Suggestions for My Top Ten:

1) Listening to my favourite music

2) Playing with my dog

3) Lying on my bed

4) Talking to my friends

5) Seeing my Nan

6) Having a dance

7) Going to my club

8) Eating a piece of cake

9) Playing my favourite computer game

10) Swimming

Appendix 8: Leaf Template

For our Network Tree:

Write your suggestions on the leaf.

This is not your network.

These are your suggestions of people

that someone could have on their network.

Appendix 9: Network Template

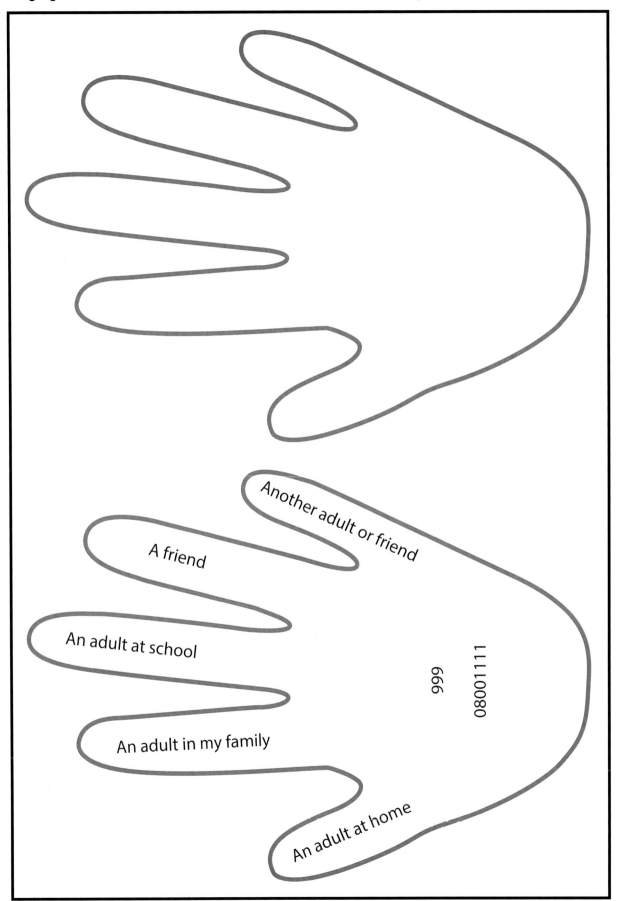

Another adult or friend

A friend

An adult at school

An adult in my family

999

08001111

An adult at home

Appendix 10: Network Bookmark

My Network

I have chosen these people to be on my network because:

- I trust them
- I feel safe with them
- I know they will try and help me

_____

_____

_____

_____

**Childline
0800 1111**

**Emergency
999**

My Network

I have chosen these people to be on my network because:

- I trust them
- I feel safe with them
- I know they will try and help me

_____

_____

_____

_____

**Childline
0800 1111**

**Emergency
999**

Appendix 11: Network Invitation

Will you be on my network?	I have chosen you to be on my network because:
	I think you will • Listen to me • Believe me • Help me to feel safe again
I have been learning about feeling safe and feeling unsafe. If I am feeling unsafe or if I am worried or sad I can talk with someone on my network. Being on my network is like being a really good friend.	An adult in my family An adult at school A friend An adult at home Another adult or friend 999 08001111

Appendix 12: Persistence Cards

When should Joe persist and when should he 'leave it'?

When Joe's friend has fallen over	When Joe is upset
When Joe wants to stay up late playing computer games	When Joe feels frightened
When Joe doesn't feel safe	When Joe wants a third helping of pudding
When Joe wants some more sweets	When Joe feels unwell
When Joe doesn't want to do his chores	When Joe ....

Appendix 13: Being a Helpful Friend

What might you say or do if your friend...

heard a nasty rumour about themselves

was being left out by some other friends

had hurt someone else's feelings

had told an adult they were being bullied but nothing had happened

knew that someone was sending nasty messages to a classmate

was being forced to do something they didn't want to do

was going to a new school without knowing anyone there

was planning to meet someone they only knew on the internet

thought it was funny to make fun of someone who was new to your school

was struggling to do their homework

Appendix 14: My Safe Safe

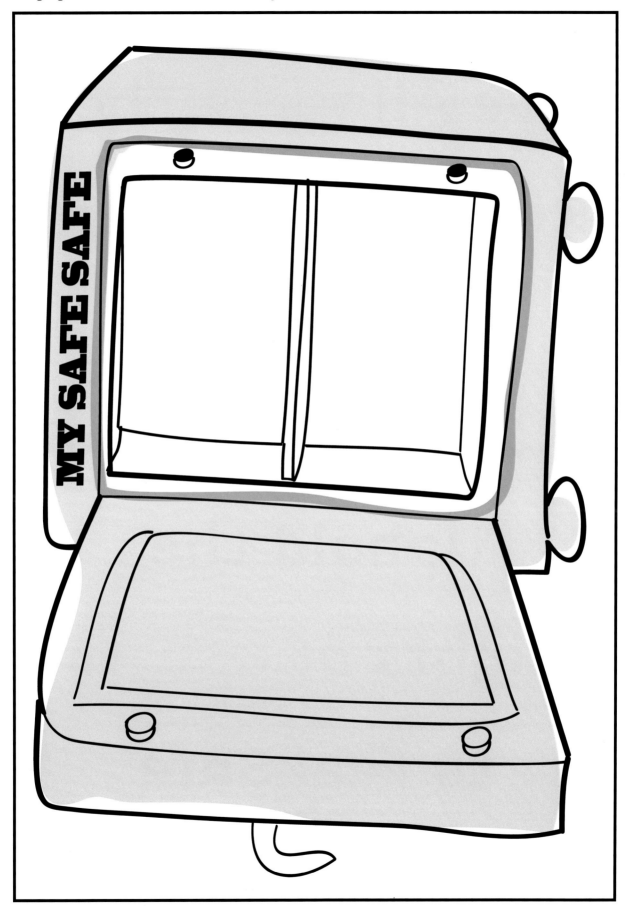

Appendix 15: Poster

We All Have the

Right to Feel Safe

and the

Responsibility to

Uphold the

Rights of Others

to Feel Safe

Appendix 16: Breathing, Relaxation and Waking Up!

Hot chocolate breathing

Imagine you have a mug of lovely hot chocolate in your hands.

Breathe in deeply through your nose as if you are smelling the chocolatey smell, for a count of 3.

And then breathe out through your mouth as though you are blowing to cool down the hot chocolate, for a count of 3.

Repeat but this time try cooling it down for a count of 4.

Then for a count of 5.

And then for a count of 6.

The longer you breathe out, the better.

Some quick relaxation techniques

Head on table.

Close eyes (if you feel safe to do so).

Scrunch up your face really tightly and breathe in … then relax it and breathe out deeply.

Scrunch up your hands into tight fists and breathe in … then relax them and breathe out deeply.

Scrunch up your toes and breathe in … then relax them and breathe out deeply.

Scrunch your shoulders up to your ears and breathe in … then relax them and breathe out deeply.

Scrunch everything up, breathing in, hold, and relax, breathing out.

You can do one or all of these 'scrunches' depending on the time you have.

Calming sounds

The sea

Wind chimes

Music: Beethoven – 6th Symphony (Pastoral)

    Brian Eno – Deep Blue Day (from Trainspotting), Space Music

    Le Mystère des voix Bulgares – Polegnala e Todora (Love Chant)

    Satie – Gymnopédies

Or if you want to change the mood entirely watch and dance to 'Lucky Chops NYC' (YouTube)!